I0815293

END TIMES

MADE EASY

Timothy Paul Jones

End Times Made Easy
Copyright © 2024 Rose Publishing

Published by Rose Publishing
An imprint of Tyndale House Ministries
Carol Stream, Illinois
www.hendricksonrose.com

The *Made Easy* series is a collection of concise, pocket-sized books that summarize key biblical teachings and provide clear, user-friendly explanations to common questions about the Christian faith. Find more *Made Easy* books at www.hendricksonrose.com.

ISBN 979-8-4005-0238-5

All rights reserved. No part of this work may be reproduced or transmitted in any form or by any means, electronic or mechanical, including photocopying, recording, or by any information storage and retrieval system, without permission in writing from the publisher.

Adapted from *Rose Guide to End Times Prophecy* by Timothy Paul Jones (Rose Publishing, 2011).

Contributing author: Timothy Paul Jones, PhD

Unless otherwise indicated, all Scriptures are taken from the Holy Bible, New International Version,® NIV.® Copyright © 1973, 1978, 1984, 2011 by Biblica, Inc.® Used by permission of Zondervan. All rights reserved worldwide. www.zondervan.com. The "NIV" and "New International Version" are trademarks registered in the United States Patent and Trademark Office by Biblica, Inc.® Scripture quotations marked NLT are taken from the Holy Bible, New Living Translation, copyright ©1996, 2004, 2015 by Tyndale House Foundation. Used by permission of Tyndale House Publishers, Carol Stream, Illinois 60188. All rights reserved.

Photos used under license from Shutterstock.com; Adobe Stock (p. 10); Unsplash (p. 47).

Printed by Regent Publishing Services Ltd.
Printed in China
May 2024, 1st printing

Contents

CHAPTER 1

Are We Living in the Last Days?

Are we living in the last days? On the one hand, this is a simple question to answer. Yes, we are! The Bible says so:

- When the Holy Spirit filled people's lives on the day of Pentecost, the apostle Peter proclaimed that this outpouring had been predicted by the Old Testament prophet Joel, and Peter identified these events as part of "the last days" (Acts 2:16–17).

- The book of Hebrews makes the point even clearer: "In these last days, he has spoken to us by his Son" (Hebrews 1:2). The work of Jesus Christ on earth was the ultimate sign of the times, and in him the last days have already dawned.

In this sense, the New Testament writers were able to describe the entire period between Jesus's resurrection and the end of time as "the last days."

On the other hand, the question "Are we living in the last days?" can actually be a bit more tricky to answer. Often when people ask this question, they're looking for answers to an array of questions about the end of time: *How soon will Jesus return? Will he come back in our lifetimes? Are the events we see in the news signs of the end of the age? What can we expect to happen in these last days?* How Christians answer these types of questions depends on how they interpret biblical prophecies and divine promises. Or more specifically, it's determined by how they view the fulfillments of God's promises; how they understand the book of Revelation and other parts of the Bible like it; and what they take Jesus's words to his disciples on the Mount of Olives to mean.

END TIMES:
Events leading up to and including the physical return of Jesus to earth and the formation of the new heavens and a new earth.

We'll look at all these things in the pages ahead, comparing the different ways Christians understand the end times. No matter what you may already think about the end times, this study can provide encouragement for your daily life.

If you feel very certain about a particular end-times view, consider this an opportunity to see what other Bible-believing Christians with different viewpoints think will happen in the last days.

If you're not sure what you believe about the end times, this book will help you sample the different views and search the Scriptures for yourself. And whichever view you land on (if any), you can still be encouraged to do what Jesus told his disciples: "Keep watch, because you do not know on what day your Lord will come" (Matthew 24:42).

If you're worried that studying the end times is too complicated, too strange, or just not worth the effort, you can use this book to dip your toe into the water and discover that God designed every detail of Scripture, even the parts about the end times, to "prepare and equip his people to do every good work" (1 Timothy 3:14 NLT).

Keeping Our Eyes on the Right End

Studying the end times might feel like dangerous business. An overemphasis on the end times, no matter how well-meaning, has been known to drive people to some peculiar behaviors. Whether it's sporting "The End Is Near!" placards on street corners or staring at barcodes in search of the mysterious mark of the beast—people sometimes worry they might find themselves veering off into hazardous end-times alleyways.

But there's one simple fact that you need to remember to keep yourself headed in the right direction: *It's only dangerous if you focus on the wrong end.*

In the gospel of John, there's a story about a time when some religious teachers questioned Jesus about his messianic credentials. Jesus replied to them, "You study the Scriptures diligently because you think that in them you have eternal life. These are the very Scriptures that testify about me" (John 5:39).

Did you catch that?

"These are," Jesus said about the Bible, "the very Scriptures that testify about me."

The Scriptures—where the religious teachers looked for life by observing religious laws and connecting themselves with patriarchs like Abraham—were not primarily about rules or family identities at all. The Scriptures were (and still are) about Jesus. That's why, when Jesus ran across a duo of downtrodden disciples on the road to Emmaus, he began "with Moses and all the Prophets" and showed them how he was the central subject of "all the Scriptures" (Luke 24:27). That's also why Paul pointed out to his pastoral protégé, Timothy, that the purpose of "the Holy Scriptures" was to make God's people "wise for salvation through faith in Christ Jesus" (2 Timothy 3:15).

ESCHATOLOGY: From the Greek word *eschaton,* meaning "final" or "last," and *logos,* meaning "word" or "idea." Eschatology is the study of the events leading up to the end of time.

The endpoint and goal of God's work in history is not a specific series of apocalyptic events or even a particular celestial place; it is, instead, a Person. It is Jesus who declared, "I am the Alpha and Omega, the First and the Last, the Beginning and the End" (Revelation 22:13). He is the source of the created order, the one "for whom and through whom everything exists" (Hebrews 2:10; Colossians 1:16). Jesus is the source of God's creation and God's story, and he is the goal of God's plan.

To be sure, God will end the world as we know it at some particular time and in a particular way—that's what we call the "end times"—but it isn't simply the termination of time for which the entire cosmos is groaning. What all creation expectantly awaits is the revealing of Jesus alongside a redeemed multitude of his followers (Romans 8:18–23). God's purpose is not simply to get people into heaven. His plan has always been to display his glory throughout the world in and through Jesus (Ephesians 1:9–10). Heaven, the new creation, and our salvation are all results of God's plan to bring everything together in Jesus the Messiah.

So, as we move forward into this study about the end times, we must, as Hebrews 12:2 says, keep our eyes fixed squarely on Jesus, the one who begins and completes our faith.

Finding Common Ground

Before we start sifting through the different end-times views, it's important to pause and consider the common ground among Christians. Here are three truths about the end times that Christians throughout history have always believed.

1. Jesus is returning.

Christians agree that Jesus will return to earth in bodily form at some point in the future, though they hold different views about the sequence of events surrounding his arrival. Some believe that Christ's return will be one single event *after* a time of tribulation. Others believe that God will remove his followers *before* a time of tribulation, and then Christ will return to reign after the tribulation has passed.

- At Christ's ascension into heaven, two angels said to the disciples, "Why do you stand here looking into the sky? This same Jesus, who has been taken from you into heaven, will come back in the same way you have seen him go into heaven" (Acts 1:10–11).
- Paul taught that "the Lord himself will come down from heaven, with a loud command, with the voice of the archangel and with the trumpet call of God, and the dead in Christ will rise first" (1 Thessalonians 4:16).

2. *Jesus will judge humanity.*

Christians agree that Jesus will judge all humanity. Some expect Jesus to judge Christians at the "judgment seat of Christ" and nonbelievers at the "great white throne," while others expect the judgment of all humanity to happen at once, believers and nonbelievers together.

- Paul wrote that "we must all appear before the judgment seat of Christ, so that each of us may receive what is due us for the things done while in the body, whether good or bad" (2 Corinthians 5:10).
- In the book of Revelation, John described this fascinating scene: "Then I saw a great white throne and him who was seated on it.... And I saw the dead, great and small, standing before the throne, and books were opened. Another book was opened, which is the book of life. The dead were judged according to what they had done as recorded in the books.... Anyone whose name was not found written in the book of life was thrown into the lake of fire" (Revelation 20:11–15).

3. *God will resurrect all people.*

Christians agree that God will physically resurrect all humanity at some point in the future. Believers differ about whether the resurrection will occur all at once at the end of time, or if some people will be resurrected before the great tribulation and some afterward, with the remainder resurrected after a thousand-year reign of Jesus on earth.

- Paul wrote about the resurrection of the dead, saying, "The body that is sown is perishable, it is raised imperishable ... it is sown a natural body, it is raised a spiritual body" (1 Corinthians 15:42–44).

- John wrote about a first resurrection and a second death: "Blessed and holy are those who share in the first resurrection. The second death has no power over them, but they will be priests of God and of Christ and will reign with him for a thousand years" (Revelation 20:6).

Throughout time and throughout the world, Christians have agreed on the three essential truths listed above—but the agreement doesn't stop there. In the opening verses of the book of Revelation, John reminds his Christian readers that he, too, shares in the experiences of their daily lives:

> *I, John, your brother and companion in the suffering and kingdom and patient endurance that are ours in Jesus....* (Revelation 1:9)

Despite the distance and differences that separated John from his readers, he was a "brother and companion" with them when it came to suffering (or tribulation), kingdom, and patient endurance.

Two thousand years later, when looking at the end times, these same themes should continue to resonate with followers of Jesus. One person may take a different view on the Antichrist or the millennium than another in their church, but when it comes to kingdom, tribulation, and patient endurance, there is far more that draws believers together than pulls them apart. Regardless of their differences, every believer in Jesus participates in God's eternal kingdom, faces times of trouble, and patiently awaits Jesus's return.

The Glory of the Kingdom

The kingdom of God consists of God's people living in God's domain under God's rule.[1] Christians in a multitude of times and places have agreed that God inaugurated a kingdom through the life, death, and resurrection of Jesus. From the very beginning of his earthly ministry, the gospel of Jesus was the good news of the kingdom of God (Matthew 3:2; 4:17, 23; 24:14). This kingdom will not be fully realized until King Jesus returns to earth, but that doesn't make the kingdom of God any less true or real.

The Reality of Tribulation

Because this Christ-inaugurated kingdom is not yet fully realized on earth, God's people still endure times of tribulation even as they rejoice in the truth of God's eternal kingdom—and this should not surprise us.

Jesus clearly predicted tribulation for his followers: "In the world you will have trouble," he said, "but take heart! I have overcome the world" (John 16:33). Until the return of Jesus Christ, God's people will experience persecution, suffering, and distress. Although many of us haven't experienced severe persecution firsthand, Christians around the world today suffer terrible persecution and martyrdom for the sake of Christ.

Throughout this long period of waiting for God's kingdom to fully come and make everything new, all creation "groans together" with God's children in expectation of a revelation that will mark the end of all suffering (Romans 8:22–23).

The Responsibility to Endure Patiently

What are Christians called to do while awaiting this revelation? Every believer in Jesus Christ is a partner with other believers, not only in kingdom and tribulation, but also in patient endurance. Until God's kingdom is fully realized, Christians wait patiently (Romans 8:25).

But this kind of patient endurance is very different from laziness or passivity. For believers in Jesus, it means working together to expand the kingdom of Christ into the lives of people around them while finding contentment in the goodness of God's providential care in each present moment. It means never ceasing to pray as Jesus taught, "Your kingdom come, your will be done, on earth as it is in the heavens" (Matthew 6:10).

The Christian life is not only about the future, the end times, or even just making it to heaven. If you are a believer in the Lord Jesus—no matter what you think about the precise timing or sequence of events in the last days—these three themes of kingdom, tribulation, and patient endurance are not simply theoretical aspects of your future life. Kingdom, tribulation, and patient endurance are woven into every moment of your life here and now.

With these truths in our minds and our eyes fixed on Jesus, let's forge ahead and examine the four main Christians views about the end times.

CHAPTER 2

What Will Happen in the End Times?

In Revelation, the last book of the Bible, the apostle John is given some amazing (and often bizarre) visions from God. In chapter 20, John glimpses a glorious angelic being. The angel bursts forth from the heavens with a chain and a key in hand. Suddenly, a dragon appears—the same dragon who had slithered into the garden of Eden as a serpent and who had whispered temptations in the Messiah's ear in the deserts of Judea. The divinely-empowered angel seizes the dragon, chains him, and hurls him into a bottomless pit where he will remain for a thousand years. Throughout this span of one thousand years, the souls of martyrs and faithful witnesses live and reign with Christ.

In Christian theology, this thousand-year reign has become known as the millennium, from the Latin terms for thousand (*mille*) and year (*annum*). This idea of a millennial kingdom can spark a lot of questions for Bible readers:

- Are the ten centuries of the millennium intended to be taken as a precise time period or rather as a symbol of something greater?
- When in human history does the chaining of Satan (the dragon) take place? Has it already happened or is this event yet to come?
- Will Jesus physically return to earth before the millennium or after?

Over the history of Christianity, four main views have developed about how time will end, and all four views involve how Bible readers understand the millennium. These views are:

- Dispensational premillennialism
- Historical premillennialism
- Amillennialism
- Postmillennialism

All four views agree on three essential truths about the end times: (1) someday Jesus will return to set the world right, (2) God will resurrect all humanity, and (3) Jesus will be their judge. Yet each view has a very different perspective on *when* Jesus will return, *when* the millennial kingdom will be established, and *how* Jesus will establish this kingdom.

Dispensational Premillennialism

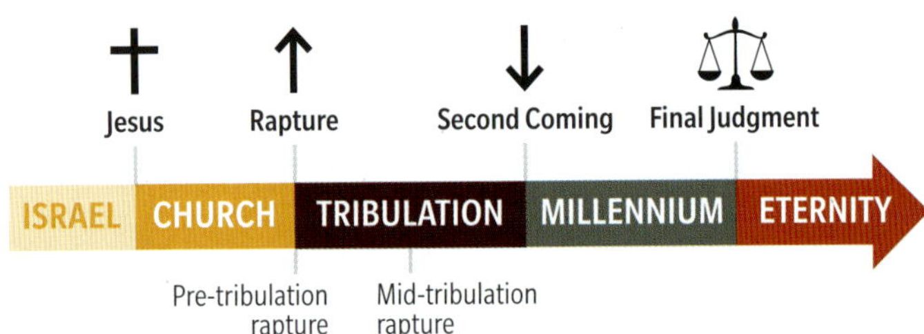

In this end-times view, known as dispensational premillennialism, Jesus Christ will return to earth before ("pre-") the millennium. But before he returns to establish his thousand-year kingdom, seven years of tribulation will afflict the earth.

The Rapture

Perhaps the most distinctive feature of this view is its teachings about the rapture. The scriptural basis for the rapture comes especially from Paul's first letter to Christians in Thessalonica. In this letter, Paul encourages the church to have hope in the resurrection of believers, because one day

> *The Lord himself will come down from heaven, with a loud command, with the voice of the archangel and with the trumpet call of God, and the dead in Christ will rise first. After that, we who are still alive and are left will be caught up together with them in the clouds to meet the Lord in the air. And so we will be with the Lord forever.* (1 Thessalonians 4:16–17)

This event of being "caught up together ... to meet the Lord" is known as the rapture. The word *rapture* does not appear in most English Bibles. Still, *rapture* is a thoroughly biblical term. In the Latin Bible, the term rendered "caught up" (or "taken up") in 1 Thessalonians is the Latin verb *rapiemur,* from the noun *raptus.* The word *rapture* simply comes from the Latin translation and means "being caught up."

Someday Jesus will return, and his people will be caught up to meet him in the air. On this point, everyone who trusts the teachings of Scripture finds common ground. But what makes dispensational premillennialism distinct is that this view sees the rapture and the second coming of Christ as two different events separated by a period of intense tribulation. (The other three end-times views understand the rapture and the return of Christ as events happening together.)

Most people who hold to dispensational premillennialism expect Christians to be raptured from the world before the tribulation begins (pre-tribulation). A few think the rapture will happen at some point partway through the tribulation (mid-tribulation or pre-wrath rapture). Either way, the rapture could happen at any time, and Jesus calls his followers to be ready always.

Israel and the Church

The rapture isn't the only distinguishing mark of dispensational premillennialism. In fact, this separation of the rapture from the second coming is actually the result of a much deeper distinction. To understand this, we need to take a careful look at the "dispensational" part of this view's name. Classical dispensationalists believe that God has always had two purposes with two distinct peoples: the nation of Israel and the church.

- One purpose has earthly objectives and involves Abraham's ethnic descendants (Israel).
- The other purpose has heavenly objectives and involves believers in Jesus (the church)

Early dispensationalists separated the rapture from the return of Christ because they believed that God had to remove his heavenly people (the church) from the world before he could resume his work with his earthly people (Israel).

Different distinguishable outworkings of God's plan in human history are known as *dispensations.* Not everyone who holds this end-times view agrees on the same number of dispensations (some count up to eight dispensations). But there are three main epochs that virtually every dispensationalist accepts:

1. During the *dispensation of Israel,* God worked primarily with the physical descendants of Abraham. The focus of this dispensation was earthly and political, centered on the promised land. (God will resume this dispensation after the rapture of the church.)

2. When the leaders of Israel rejected Jesus as the Messiah, God postponed the promised kingdom and instituted the *dispensation of the church.* During this time, God is drawing believing Jews and gentiles together into one body—the church. The focus of this new dispensation is spiritual. This is the dispensation we're living in today.

3. After the second coming, Christ will reign over all earth with ethnic Israelites in his thousand-year millennial kingdom. Paul describes this *millennial dispensation* in Ephesians 1:10: "... to be put into effect when the times reach their fulfillment—to bring unity to all things in heaven and on earth under Christ."

Dispensationalists see God's covenant with Abraham in Genesis as including unconditional guarantees of land and blessings for Abraham's descendants. God called this covenant an "everlasting covenant" (Genesis 17:7, 13, 19). Because this covenant is unconditional and everlasting, God must still fulfill his promises to Israel's first father—and this fulfillment must meet the expectations of the first hearers of this promise. Despite Israel's constant disobedience throughout the Old and New Testaments, "it is not as though the word of God had failed" (Romans 9:6). Dispensationalists expect that at some point before the end of time, the Jewish people will thrive in the land that stretches from the Euphrates River to the Nile River and thereby bless the rest of the world (Genesis 12:2–3; 15:18). God will fulfill his everlasting covenant and give the promised land to the nation of Israel.

NOTABLE DISPENSATIONAL PREMILLENNIALISTS

- John Nelson Darby, 19th-century British Bible Teacher, the "father of dispensationalism"
- C. I. Scofield, 19th-century American theologian
- More recently, John MacArthur, Tim LaHaye, David Jeremiah

AN ANCIENT COVENANT AND THE FUTURE OF THE WORLD

One day, some four thousand years ago, God called an idol-worshiper named Abraham to pack his bags, leave his homeland, and head to a land that God would reveal to him later (Genesis 12:1). The blessings that awaited Abraham and his family were incredible.

- **Innumerable descendants:** Abraham's offspring would multiply into a great nation (Genesis 12:2).
- **Land:** His descendants would inherit a specific land—the promised land (Genesis 13:15).
- **Worldwide blessing:** One particular offspring would be the means by which God would bless the whole world (Genesis 18:10, 18).

Abraham followed God's call to go to the promised land, and God made a covenant with him. The word *covenant* comes from the Hebrew word *berit,* which may come from another Hebrew word meaning "to bind." Ancient covenants were binding promises which required personal trust between the parties involved.

God's covenant with Abraham plays a central role in God's plan for the world. These divine promises pulse like a wave through the rest of the biblical story. This ripple begins in Genesis and runs through Revelation.

So what does this covenant have to do with the end of time?

Everything!

The nation of Israel arose from God's promises to Abraham, who was the ancestor of the Jewish people. In Old Testament prophecy, Israel is central; on this point, Christians agree. But past this point, differences begin to emerge: Were God's promises to Israel fulfilled at some point in Old Testament times? Were the promises primarily fulfilled through one particular Israelite, a descendant of Abraham known as Jesus of Nazareth? Are the promises being fulfilled through the church today? Will the promises be fulfilled through the nation of Israel at some point in the future? How someone answers these questions makes a big difference for what one expects to happen in the end times.

"I will make you into a great nation, and I will bless you; I will make your name great, and you will be a blessing. I will bless those who bless you, and whoever curses you I will curse; and all peoples on earth will be blessed through you."

Genesis 12:1–3; see also
Genesis 13:14–17; 15:1–20; 17:1–8

The Tribulation and the Return of Jesus

So, what exactly is it that dispensational premillennialists believe will happen near the end of time? Of course there are a handful of differences among people who hold this end-times view, but most agree on a similar sequence of events surrounding the time of the tribulation:

- Before the tribulation, the nation of Israel will sign a treaty (the "strong covenant" in Daniel 9:27) with a world leader who is "the beast," the Antichrist (Revelation 11:7; 13:1–8; 1 John 2:18). The Antichrist will assist in rebuilding the temple in Jerusalem.

- The ratification of this treaty will begin the seven-year tribulation. But before this, God will remove his church from the world through the rapture (1 Thessalonians 4:16–17). The seven years of tribulation are the "seventieth seven" predicted by the Old Testament prophet Daniel (Daniel 9:24).

- Near the beginning of the tribulation, God will designate 144,000 Jewish believers in Jesus to proclaim the gospel. Through their testimony, many will trust in Jesus (Revelation 7:4–17).

- Halfway through the tribulation, the Antichrist will break his treaty with Israel and desecrate the temple (Daniel 9:27). Some dispensationalists believe the rapture will happen around this time instead of placing the rapture prior to the tribulation.

- In the final forty-two months (three and a half years) of the tribulation, persecution will increase (Revelation 13:5). This is the "great tribulation" that Jesus described to his disciples on the Mount of Olives (Matthew 24:21).
- Armies of the world will array themselves against the Jewish people at a place known as Armageddon (Revelation 16:16).
- Israel will repent and recognize Jesus as their Messiah (Hosea 5:15–6:3).
- Jesus will return to earth and defeat his enemies, bind Satan, and reign from Jerusalem for one thousand calendar years. At the end of this millennial reign, Satan will be released, defeated, and forever consigned to the lake of fire (Revelation 20:7–15).

You may not agree with the dispensational premillennial perspective; and even if you would never consider sticking an "In Case of Rapture, This Car Will Be Unoccupied" decal on your vehicle's bumper, there is much you can appreciate about this end-times view. Virtually without exception, dispensationalists believe the Bible to constitute unfailing truth without any mixture of error, and it should be studied in earnest. Most are driven to their end-times views because they truly want to trust and obey what the text of Scripture says.

This end-times view emphasizes the need to be ready and to proclaim the gospel *now*. Christians could be removed from the world at any moment, so now is the time to prepare our hearts and to speak the gospel into the lives of people around us. As Paul said, "Now is the time of God's favor, now is the day of salvation" (2 Corinthians 6:2).

Historical Premillennialism

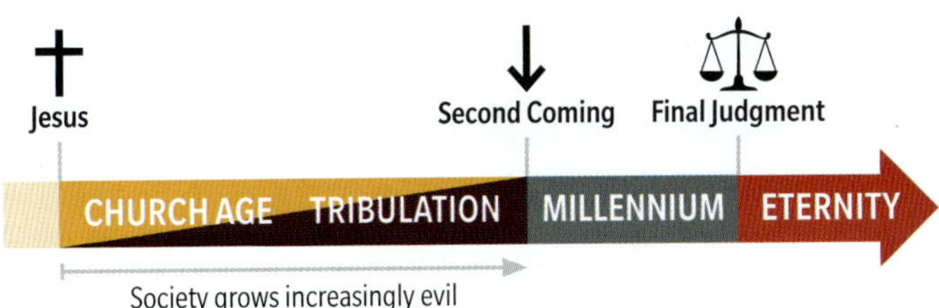

The next end-times view we'll look at is also a premillennial view. It's called historical premillennialism. Like its dispensational variety, this view teaches that the second coming of Christ will happen before ("pre-") the millennium, but beyond that, it's a very different perspective on the end times.

Dispensationalists expect the church to make a secret exit off the face of planet earth before the worst trials and tribulations fall upon the world, but historical premillennialists expect that Christians will be "caught up" (or "raptured," 1 Thessalonians 4:16–17) immediately before the second coming of Christ to the earth when he establishes his millennial kingdom. Therefore, the church will remain on earth throughout the tribulation.

Those who hold this view point out that in 2 Thessalonians Paul said that, at the second coming, Jesus will:

- "give relief" to his church (1:7);
- destroy "the lawless one" (2:8);
- be "revealed from heaven in blazing fire with his powerful angels" (1:7); and
- "punish those who do not know God and who do not obey the gospel of our Lord Jesus" (1:8).

Paul did not separate the "relief" God's people will experience when they are "caught up" from the judgment Jesus will bring when he returns to earth. Paul seems to portray Christians being "caught up together" and Christ's return as two parts of one, single glorious "coming of our Lord Jesus Christ" (2 Thessalonians 2:1).

The Covenant Fulfilled

But the timing of the rapture isn't the only difference between the two premillennial views. The deepest divergence has to do with how each group views the relationship between the nation of Israel and the church.

Dispensationalists organize God's work into dispensations, and in each dispensation God works in a particular way with a particular purpose. God's activities with Israel and with the church occur as parts of two different dispensations.

Historical premillennialists, however, believe that God's plan has always been to create *one* people for his glory through the death and resurrection of Jesus (Ephesians 2:15). All God's work with the nation of Israel in the Old Testament was a preparation for and a picture of what God had already purposed to do through Jesus. God's true people in every age—whether in Old Testament or New Testament times, whether Jews or gentiles—has been those who live by faith in Jesus as the divine Messiah-King (Hebrews 11:13, 39–40). God is fulfilling the promises he made to Israel through Jesus. During the millennial kingdom, Jesus will reign from Jerusalem, not only over the land promised to Abraham, but also over the whole earth. King Jesus, the rightful ruler of Israel, will reign over every inch of real estate that God promised to Israel and so much more. Therefore, during the millennium, Jesus will completely fulfill every promise of God.

So does this mean that according to historical premillennialists the Jewish people no longer have a special place in God's plan? Certainly not! The preservation of the Jewish people to this present time is seen as a miraculous sign of God's continuing presence in the world. As novelist Walker Percy has pointed out, "[There are] no Hittites walking about on the streets of New York"—but there are millions of descendants of the ancient Israelites![2]

Many historical premillennialists anticipate that at some point before the return of Christ there will be a widespread spiritual awakening among the Jewish people. Throughout the world, Jews will turn to Jesus as their Messiah, Savior, and God. That's what Paul was predicting when he wrote that Israel would remain resistant to the gospel only "until the fullness of the Gentiles has come in" (Romans 11:25). The primary focus of God's promises is not the physical land of Israel but the divine person of Jesus who will reign over the land of Israel when he rules over the whole earth from Jerusalem. What historical premillennialists anticipate for the Jewish people is not the restoration of the modern nation of Israel to a particular piece land but numerous Jews turning to Jesus. Because of this expectation, there is every reason to proclaim the good news about Jesus "to the Jew first" (Romans 1:16).

The Tribulation

Historical premillennialists believe that the church remains on earth during the tribulation. But when will this tribulation begin and how long will it last?

Some understand the tribulation to be a relatively brief period that will occur near the end of time. If the forty-two months in Revelation 11:2 refer to the same period as the forty-two months in Revelation 13:5, the tribulation will last only three and a half years (one "forty-two months"). If these two periods are different, then the span of the tribulation will be seven years (two "forty-two months").

Others take the forty-two months as a symbolic reference drawn from other biblical imagery: the encampments of Israel in the wilderness (Numbers 33:5–29) and the months of drought during the ministry of Elijah (Luke 4:25; James 5:17). If the months are symbolic, then the tribulation could be a very long period that began in the first century and continues until the second coming of Christ.

One Final Point

Now that we've covered the basics of this end-times view, you might be left with one nagging question: *What's so "historical" about historical premillennialism anyway?* This view is the earlier and older (the "historical") form of premillennialism. (Another name for historical premillennialism is *chiliasm.*) Historical premillennial teachings can be found in the writings of early church leaders such as Papias, a disciple of the apostle John; Justin Martyr, one of the first Christian apologists; Irenaeus of Lyons, a student of Polycarp who was a disciple of the apostle John; and Tertullian, a second-century North African theologian. In their writings, they seem to place the millennium after the resurrection of the dead and expect that Christians will face suffering as the "beast antichrist" wages war upon the church of God.[3]

Whether or not you believe the church endures the tribulation, historical premillennialism reminds us how God constantly uses day-by-day trials to move his people toward maturity:

- According to Paul, Christians must not merely tolerate the tribulations of this life but must see these trials as opportunities for God to purify and transform his people (Romans 5:3–5; 12:12; 2 Corinthians 6:4–5).

- Barnabas and Paul testified together that it is only through many tribulations that we enter God's kingdom (Acts 14:22). Paul even declared that Christians are "destined" for tribulation (1 Thessalonians 3:3).

- Jesus predicted that believers would endure times of grief and pain (John 16:21–22), and he made it clear that his followers would be "in the world" facing troubles (John 16:33).

All Christians can agree that even in times of suffering, trials, and tribulations—whenever they happen and however long they may last—God will faithfully preserve and protect the souls of those who truly belong to him.

NOTABLE HISTORICAL PREMILLENNIALISTS

- Charles Spurgeon, 19th-century preacher
- Carl F. H. Henry, 20th-century American theologian
- More recently, Russell Moore, D. A. Carson, John Piper

Amillennialism

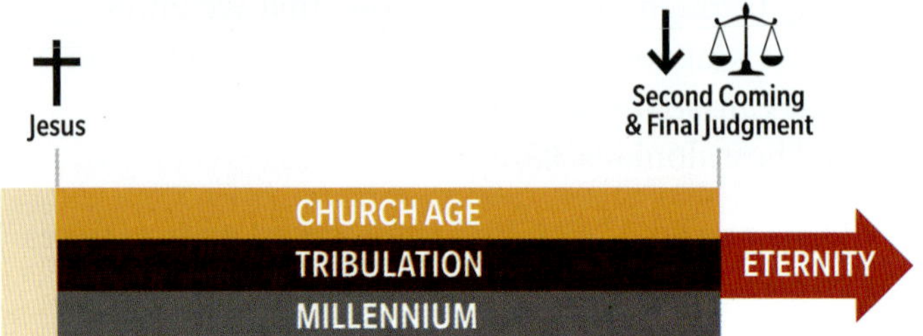

In the term *amillennial,* the prefix "a-" means "not" or "no," suggesting that amillennialists might not believe in a millennium at all. This is unfortunate, because amillennialists do in fact believe in a very real millennial reign. The difference is simply that, while the other three end-times views see the millennium as an earthly event yet to come, amillennialists see the millennial kingdom as a present spiritual reality. In other words, the millennium symbolizes the present and ongoing reign of Jesus with his people. It is a spiritual reign that extends from the first century, when Jesus won the victory over Satan, to Jesus's glorious return at the end of time. In this view, the millennial kingdom, the church age, and the tribulation are all happening at the same time.

A Thousand Years

"But wait," you might be thinking, *"how can the millennium be a present reality that began when*

Jesus ascended into heaven, when it's already been almost two thousand years since then?" From the amillennialist viewpoint, numbers in the book of Revelation are symbols, not statistics. Therefore, the thousand years of the millennium was never meant to describe a literal, specific time span. Instead, the phrase "thousand years" in Revelation symbolizes the great length and the glorious magnitude of the Messiah's present reign in the heavens. (See Ezekiel 47:3–5 for an example of a prophecy that uses "one thousand" to symbolize a great magnitude.)

Tribulations

Through the cross and the empty tomb, Jesus has already stripped Satan of his power, but the fulfillment of his reign has not yet been fully realized. Within God's sovereign purposes and plan, Satan's power is restrained but not obliterated. That's why suffering and sorrow have occurred and will continue to occur throughout the time between the triumph of Jesus on the cross and his glorious return in the future. God's kingdom is present here and now, but pain and sorrow continue. Alongside the growth and expansion of the kingdom of God, a kingdom of darkness persists—though it persists towards its ultimate defeat.

Here's how amillennialists see the future unfolding:

- Right now, Jesus is reigning with his saints in a heavenly millennial kingdom, even as tribulation continues to afflict the earth (Colossians 1:13; Revelation 20:2–6).
- Near the end of time, Satan will be allowed for a short time to deceive the nations again (Revelation 20:7–8).
- In the second coming, Jesus will call every Christian—living or dead—to meet him in the clouds (1 Thessalonians 4:16–17). Then, Jesus will immediately reveal himself on the earth, destroying every devilish resistance to his reign. All the world will see that Satan has been defeated. Jesus will judge humanity and cosign to "everlasting destruction" anyone who has not confessed Jesus as Lord (2 Thessalonians 1:7–10).
- After the final judgment, God will re-create the heavens and the earth. His holy city will descend from the heavens to the earth (Isaiah 65:17; 66:22; Revelation 21:1–8).

The church is comprised of Jews and gentiles alike, but the promises of land given to Abraham and Israel do not feature prominently in this end-times view. That's because, according to this view, God already fulfilled his promises of land to Israel (Joshua 21:43; 23:14; 1 Kings 4:20–21; 8:56).

You may not accept amillennialism as the best view of the end times. If so, that's okay! Even if you find some other end-times view more convincing, amillennialism reminds Christians of an important theme in the Bible: *Jesus has already won.* To be sure, there are still trials and tribulations. Yet through Jesus's perfect life, sacrificial death, and glorious resurrection, he has shattered Satan's power and won an ever-present kingdom for God's glory. Final victory is only a matter of time.

NOTABLE AMILLENNIALISTS

- Augustine of Hippo, 5th-century church father
- Martin Luther and John Calvin, 16th-century Reformers
- More recently, J. I. Packer, Herschel Hobbs, Kim Riddlebarger

Postmillennialism

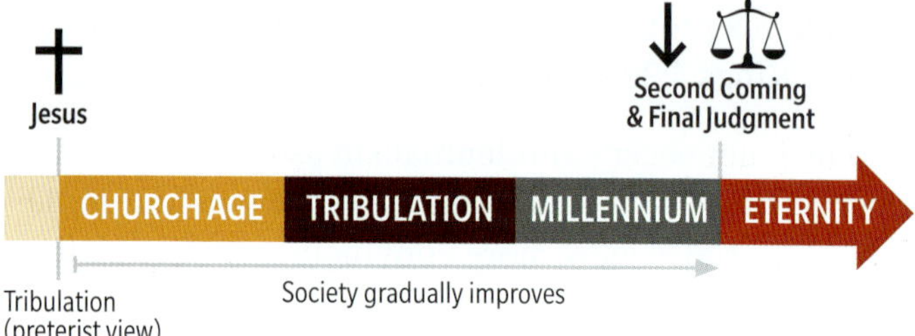

This end-times view is called postmillennialism, because in this view Christ will return to earth after ("post-") the millennium.

The Gospel and the Kingdom

According to postmillennialists, there will come a time when worldwide acceptance of the gospel ushers in the millennial kingdom. An overwhelming number of people throughout the world will trust in Jesus during this time. The vast majority of gentiles will turn to Jesus, and the Jewish people in particular will recognize him as their long-awaited Messiah (Romans 11:13–25). Entire countries and civilizations will change as citizens and leaders alike embrace the good news of the gospel. Satan will be restrained, war will give way to peace, and the saints of God will rule the nations (Revelation 20:2–6).

Jesus declared that the kingdom of God was like a tiny seed growing into a large tree and like a small amount of yeast affecting dough (Matthew 13:31–33). What this suggests to postmillennialists is that the millennial kingdom will emerge slowly and then expand to fill the entire world.

This millennium may last exactly one thousand years, or a thousand years may symbolize an extended era of gospel peace. In either case, Jesus will not be physically present on the earth during the millennium. He will instead reign spiritually through the power and proclamation of the gospel.

At the end of this glorious period, God will allow Satan to deceive the nations for a very brief time (Revelation 20:7–9). When the Satan-inspired armies of the earth have arrayed themselves against the reign of God, Jesus will finally return to earth to defeat Satan once and for all (Revelation 20:10–15). (Postmillennialists interpret the "first resurrection" in Revelation 20:5 as the spiritual regeneration that occurs in the life of every follower of Jesus, not a physical restoration from the dead; see Ephesians 2:6).

The Great Tribulation

If everything is getting better, where does the realities of suffering, trials, and tribulation fit into such an optimistic end-times view? After all, the book of

Revelation contains many visions about disasters and violence in the world. In chapter 7, John sees a great multitude wearing white robes who "have come out of the great tribulation" (verses 9, 14). Jesus, too, warned his disciples on the Mount of Olives that days are coming when there will be "days of distress unequaled from the beginning, when God created the world, until now—and never to be equaled again" (Mark 13:19). Postmillennialists don't disagree with this. They see a time of great tribulation that happens before the coming of the millennial kingdom, but they differ on exactly when and how this takes place.

Some believe that a portion (or perhaps even all) of the great tribulation occurred in the first century, either around the time of Jesus's ascension into heaven or a few decades later when Roman army destroyed the Jewish temple in Jerusalem in AD 70. If the Jewish war against the Romans that lasted from AD 66 until around AD 73 was the great tribulation, the dawning of the millennial kingdom would have begun in the first century and has continually expanded with the preaching of the gospel, and this will continue until the good news of Jesus fills the entire earth.

Other postmillennialists take a different perspective and see the great tribulation either as something presently occurring today to one extent or another, or perhaps as an event that will occur in the future.

Whenever this great tribulation ends, the millennial kingdom will begin.

The Church and the Promises of God

The nation of Israel is not emphasized in the postmillennial view. That's because most who hold this view understand the promises God made to Israel in the Old Testament as either already fulfilled or currently fulfilled through the church. They see covenantal continuity between Israel and the church.

Here's how postmillennialists might understand some key passages of Scripture:

- In Paul's letter to the Galatians, he emphasizes that Jesus Christ is Abraham's one "offspring" or one "seed," the perfect covenant-keeping Israelite (Galatians 3:7–9, 13–14, 16). Faith in Jesus is what brings together Jews and gentiles to inherit the promises given to Abraham.

- In the Old and New Testaments alike, salvation came through faith in Jesus as Lord and Messiah. Old Testament believers looked forward to the Messiah with expectant faith (Hebrews 11:13, 39–40) and New Testament believers look back to Jesus Christ. God has always had one plan with one people. There is only one covenant of grace, which stretches from Adam and Eve in garden of Eden to the triumph of Jesus Christ at the end of time.

And what about the land that was promised to Abraham?

- Some postmillennialists believe the promise of land have already been fulfilled in the establishment of Israel in the region of Canaan through Joshua's conquest (Joshua 11:23; 21:43–45; Nehemiah 9:22–25) or possibly later in Israel's history during King Solomon's reign (1 Kings 4:21; 5:4). If so, no literal earthly millennium is necessary for God to keep his word to Israel.

- Others believe that God's promise was conditional, and so Abraham's descendants forfeited the promise by rebelling against God and rejecting his Messiah, Jesus Christ (Matthew 21:43).

- Still others say the work and growth of the church is an ongoing fulfillment of God's promises to Abraham and Israel in the Old Testament as God reigns over ever-increasing numbers of people through the gospel. (See Paul's reference to followers of Jesus as "the Israel of God" in Galatians 6:16.)

Postmillennialism is clearly an end-times perspective that highlights the power of the gospel. This emphasis on the gospel should remind every Christian to be passionate about how the good news of Jesus can transform people's lives.

Regardless of your end-times viewpoint, it is possible to embrace the belief that the gospel really can change entire communities, cultures, and even the world. In this sense, the gospel is far more than the initial statement that helps someone understand how to confess Jesus as the risen Lord—although such statements are certainly important! It's also a constant reminder that, in every moment of our lives, we desperately need what God has provided in the crucified and risen Christ. Whatever problems we face—whatever tribulations come our way—the gospel forms the foundation for God's solution. That's the true power of the gospel. And, even if you're not a postmillennialist, that's good news.

NOTABLE POSTMILLENNIALISTS

- Jonathan Edwards, 18th-century Great Awakening preacher
- B. B. Warfield, 19th-century American theologian
- More recently, Loraine Boettner, R.C. Sproul, R. J. Rushdoony

DISPENSATIONAL PREMILLENNIALISM	
When will Jesus return?	Jesus will return before the tribulation.
What is the tribulation?	The tribulation is a seven-year period of worldwide suffering. The church will be raptured out of the world either before the tribulation or half-way through the tribulation.
What is the millennium?	The millennium is a literal one-thousand year reign of Christ from Jerusalem that will begin after the tribulation.

HISTORICAL PREMILLENNIALISM	
When will Jesus return?	Jesus will return after the tribulation and before the millennium.
What is the tribulation?	Either the tribulation will be a time of severe oppression before the return of Jesus, lasting three and a half years or seven years, or the tribulation has been a present reality ever since the first century AD.
What is the millennium?	The millennium is the reign of Jesus from Jerusalem over the whole earth for a thousand years, which fulfills God's promises to Israel.

AMILLENNIALISM	
When will Jesus return?	Jesus could return at any time.
What is the tribulation?	Tribulation occurs any time Christians are persecuted and whenever wars and disasters happen. Christians will endure tribulations until Jesus returns.
What is the millennium?	The millennium is the present spiritual reign of Jesus with his people. It began from the time of Christ in the first century to the present day, and it will continue until Jesus returns.

POSTMILLENNIALISM	
When will Jesus return?	Jesus will return after the millennium when the power of the gospel reaches throughout the world.
What is the tribulation?	(1) The tribulation was the wars and violence that people in first-century Israel experienced; or (2) the tribulation presently occurs whenever the gospel is opposed and Christians are persecuted.
What is the millennium?	(1) The millennium will be one-thousand years of gospel peace in the future; or (2) the millennium is a present reality and "one thousand" symbolizes an extended period of time.

CHAPTER 3

What Is the Book of Revelation About?

Even if you haven't read through every book in the Bible, one thing becomes quite clear when you open your Bible to the book of Revelation: it's very different from the others.

The book of Revelation refers to historical events and places, like Babylon and the temple in Jerusalem, but not in the same way as historical books like the Gospels or the book of Acts.

Revelation begins with seven letters to seven churches in Asia Minor, yet these letters from the hand of the apostle John aren't anything like the epistles that Paul or Peter sent to churches; for that matter, they aren't even like John's other three letters in the New Testament!

APOCALYPTIC LITERATURE:
From the Greek word *apokalypsis,* meaning "revelation" or "unhiding." This genre of ancient Jewish literature is presented in the form of visions that figuratively unveil hidden truths. The term *apokalypsis* also happens to be the first word in the Greek text of the book of Revelation.

So why is Revelation so different? It's partly because its author drew from an ancient literary genre known as apocalyptic literature. These writings are filled with visions that reveal hidden truths in figurative language to bring assurance to God's people during times of suffering and persecution. This style of writing expresses both hope and lament: hope in God's sovereign rule over his world coupled with lament over the many ways that sin distorts God's good design for his world.

One of the best examples of apocalyptic writings in the Old Testament is found in the book of Daniel. In chapters 7–12, the prophet Daniel is given a series of fascinating visions.

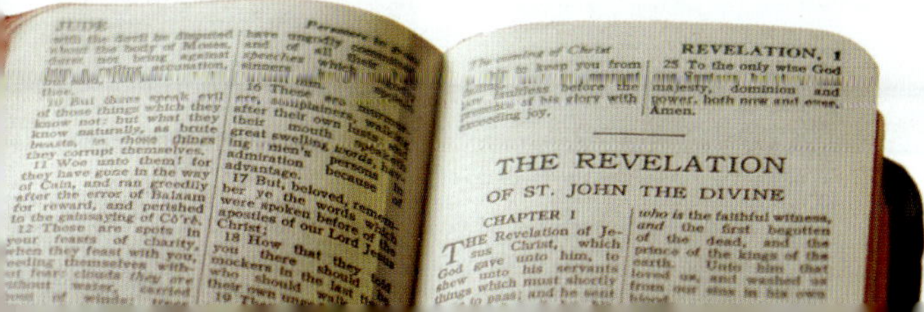

Many Bible scholars see significant parallels between the books of Daniel and Revelation.

DANIEL	REVELATION
A little horn with human eyes and a mouth that speaks boastfully (7:8)	A ten-horned beast which speaks proud words and blasphemies (13:1, 5–6; also 12:3; 17:3)
The little horn waging war against the holy people (7:21)	A ten-horned beast waging war against God's holy people (13:7)
Beasts from the sea that resemble a lion, a bear, and a leopard (7:4–6)	A beast from the sea that looks like a leopard with the feet of a bear and a mouth like a lion (13:2)
One "like a son of man" coming with the clouds of heaven (7:13)	Seated on a white cloud, one "like a son of man" with a crown of gold and sickle to harvest the earth (14:14)

Beast from the Sea (Augsburg Book of Miracles, c. 1552)

The Seven "Sevens" of Revelation

Before we go any farther down the road of figuring out what the wild visions of Revelation might mean, let's first take a quick tour through the seven "sevens" that provide the book with its internal structure. Revelation features seven cycles, each consisting of sevens things.

The Seven Churches
REVELATION 1:1–3:22

John sees a vision of the risen Christ clothed in glory and majesty in heaven. He instructs John to write seven messages to seven churches, all in cities in Asia Minor (in modern-day Turkey). These letters contain not only exhortations for the churches to repent but also encouragements for them to "hold fast" and stay strong.

2 The Seven Seals
REVELATION 4:1–8:5

Next, John sees a scroll with seven seals. As the seals are opened, John witnesses four horses (white, red, black, and pale yellow) whose riders bring great turmoil upon the earth. John also sees 144,000 servants of God sealed with divine protection and a great multitude clothed in white robes.

3 Seven Trumpets

REVELATION 8:6–11:19

When the seven trumpets are blown, natural disasters are unleashed upon the world: hail, fire, locusts, fallen stars, darkened sun and moon. The angel tells John about two witnesses from God who will be martyred by a "beast from the Abyss" and then be resurrected.

4 Seven Histories

REVELATION 12:1–14:20

Next, the focus shifts from judgment to several amazing scenes played out with an assortment of characters. These histories include a pregnant woman "clothed with the sun" who is persecuted by a dragon, but the dragon is "hurled to the earth." There are also two beasts, one from the sea and the other from the earth. Together, they deceive the world and force everyone to receive a mark, which is the name or number of the beast: 666. John then sees the Lamb standing on Mount Zion with 144,000 people redeemed from the earth. Finally, John sees one "like a son of man" harvesting the earth.

5 Seven Bowls of Judgment
REVELATION 15:1–16:21

Seven angels pour out seven bowls filled with God's wrath against his enemies and the enemies of his people. These plagues include painful sores, water turned to blood, darkness, drought, and demonic spirits gathering the kings of the earth for a battle at Armageddon.

6 Seven Messages of Judgment
REVELATION 17:1–19:10

More judgments come in the form of seven announcements describing the force of God against evil. John sees a prostitute sitting on a scarlet beast. The woman represents the great and evil city of Babylon. When Babylon falls, the merchants of the land and sea wail, but the multitude in heaven rejoices.

7 Seven Visions
REVELATION 19:11–22:21

In John's final visions, he witnesses mighty displays of God's salvation, judgment, and authority over all the earth. These visions include a rider on a white horse, a great heavenly banquet, a thousand-year reign (the millennium), thrones of judgment, Satan cast into the lake of fire, and a new heaven and a new earth with a new Jerusalem coming down from heaven.

Four Ways to Read Revelation

So what can we possibly make from all these strange and amazing visions? What do they mean?

How we interpret the visions in Revelation has a lot to do with how we approach apocalyptic texts. In other words, *what* we believe we're reading influences *how* we read it. Consider this: you probably approach the articles in your local newspaper very differently from a long classic novel. You expect the newspaper to quickly inform you about current events, while a good novel you expect to provoke questions deep in your soul through an imaginative story.

When it comes to biblical apocalypses, the same is true. How you read these writings depends on what you think you are reading and what you expect these texts to do.

- If you take the book of Revelation primarily as a book of predictions of events yet to come, you will scour the text for clues about what could happen in the future.

- But if you see Revelation mostly as an elaborate illustration of trials that Christians face in every age, you'll probably look for connections between your present struggles and the temptations of past believers.
- If you take the book as providing a God-centered perspective on historical events that were happening at the time John was writing it, you'll spend your time seeking hints of first-century happenings.

With that in mind, let's take a look at the four main ways that Christians approach the book of Revelation, along with some examples of what each approach gains from this inspired text.

Futurist View

If you see Revelation (and other apocalyptic parts of the Bible) mostly as a road map or a GPS that tells you what will happen on the road ahead of you in time, you're probably taking what's known as a *futurist* view. This approach treats the scenes in Revelation as predictive prophecies about events that, even now, have not yet occurred. The emphasis of futurism is on things that will happen near the end of time. Reading Revelation in this way can help us to look diligently at the future and to be ready for events leading up to the second coming of Christ.

Revelation is like a road map to the future.

Premillennialists tend to look at most of Revelation from this futurist viewpoint. The judgments and world events in Revelation 4–19 are understood as things that will happen in the future, before or during the seven-year tribulation. Almost every view of the end times sees Revelation as at least *partly* a description of the future.

Here are some examples of how reading Revelation from this perspective might look:

- In Revelation 7 and 14, the 144,000 people are understood to be Jewish believers—12,000 virgin men from each tribe of Israel—chosen to be witnesses during the first forty-two months of the seven-year tribulation. They will become believers during this half of the tribulation and be "sealed" and sent out as evangelists. About halfway through the tribulation, they will be killed for their faith.[4]

- In Revelation 12, in the story of the pregnant woman persecuted by the ten-horned dragon, the woman represents the nation of Israel. The dragon is Satan, who will be hurled down to earth to renew his persecution of the modern state of Israel during the seven-year tribulation: "The great dragon was hurled down—that ancient serpent called the devil, or Satan, who leads the whole world astray" (Revelation 12:9).

- In Revelation 13, the dragon (Satan) gives power to the beast from the sea, and the earthly beast performs great signs causing people to worship the beast from the sea. The beast from the sea represents the Antichrist, a future world leader during the great tribulation who will command the allegiance of many. The beast from the earth is the false prophet, a religious figure who will lead many to bow down to the Antichrist as well as urging them to receive the mark of the beast (666).

WHO IS THE ANTICHRIST?

Did you know that the term *Antichrist* never appears in the book of Revelation? But John did employ this term in his other writings, in the epistles of 1 and 2 John:

> *As you have heard that the antichrist is coming, even now many antichrists have come.... Who is the liar? It is whoever denies that Jesus is the Christ. Such a person is the antichrist—denying the Father and the Son.* (1 John 2:18–22; also 2 John 1:7)

> *Every spirit that does not acknowledge Jesus is not from God. This is the spirit of the antichrist, which you have heard is coming and even now is already in the world.* (1 John 4:3)

In this sense of the word, there were (and are) many antichrists, because the antichrist is anyone and any idea that opposes essential truths about Jesus Christ.

The apostle Paul doesn't use the word *antichrist* in his writings, but he does describe a "man of lawlessness" who will be revealed before the second coming. Many Bible readers identify this unnamed man as being the Antichrist. Paul writes that the second coming will not happen until

> *the rebellion occurs and the man of lawlessness is revealed, the man doomed*

> *to destruction. He will oppose and will exalt himself over everything that is called God or is worshiped, so that he sets himself up in God's temple, proclaiming himself to be God.* (2 Thessalonians 2:3–4)

Paul goes on to explain that

> *the lawless one will be revealed, whom the Lord Jesus will overthrow with the breath of his mouth and destroy by the splendor of his coming. The coming of the lawless one will be in accordance with how Satan works. He will use all sorts of displays of power through signs and wonders that serve the lie, and all the ways that wickedness deceives those who are perishing.* (2 Thessalonians 2:8–10)

The beast from the sea in Revelation 13 is often thought to be the Antichrist or the man of lawlessness in Paul's writings. In John's vision, this beast has a fatal wound which is miraculously healed, and the beast's number is "the number of a man. That number is 666." He marks the inhabitants of the earth on their right hands and foreheads with his number (Revelation 13:12, 18).

This number has led to all sorts of speculations throughout history about the Antichrist's identity. In retrospect, lots of these suppositions may seem ridiculous—and that should be all the more reason for us today to be very cautious about claiming to know who the Antichrist is.

A few proposed candidates for the Antichrist have included:

- Roman Emperor Nero: He persecuted Christians, and when "Nero Caesar" in Greek is transliterated into Hebrew letters, the numeric values of the Hebrew letters add up to 666. (Hebrew letters were also used as numbers.)
- Napoleon Bonaparte: In the novel *War and Peace,* one of the characters converts *L'Empereur Napoleon* into a series of numbers that add up to 666.
- Mikhail Gorbachev: He was a Soviet leader with a mysterious birthmark on his head.
- Ronald Wilson Reagan: His first, middle, and last names each had six letters. Plus, he recovered from a gunshot wound that seemed fatal.

Historicist View

If you believe apocalyptic texts prophetically provide information about a long period of history—perhaps the whole of Christian history or some other significant epoch—then you're reading Revelation from a *historicist* approach.

Revelation is like a textbook about the past, present, and future.

Historicism treats apocalyptic writings as symbolic retellings of certain eras of history. Revelation uses lavish language and elaborate visions to tell the history of Christianity, the rise and fall of the Roman Empire, or perhaps another series of events in human history since the time of Christ. John's visions, therefore, told of things that were future for him and are past (or mostly past) for us today. Reading the book of Revelation from this view can help us better understand God's perspective on the events of human history.

Some premillennialists see the letters to the seven churches at the beginning of Revelation as representing successive stages of church history.

Here are examples of how someone reading from the historicist perspective might interpret parts of the book of Revelation:

- The seven churches in Revelation 1–3 represent seven eras of church history. These letters chronologically tell the story of Christianity symbolically through seven epochs.
- The seven seals in Revelation 6 may be the stages of church history from the late first century to the late fourth century, and the seven trumpets in chapter 8 are the stages of the church from about the year 400 to the fifteenth century—or to the present.

Idealist View

If all the visions seem to you to be symbolic descriptions of the struggles God's people face in every age, then you might be looking at Revelation from an *idealist* perspective.

Revelation is a compass that directs our attention to God's sovereignty in every time and place.

In this view, Revelation is like a drama with characters and events that are symbolic expressions of the struggle between good and evil which occur at any time. The visions are, therefore, picturesque expressions of the ongoing conflict between the kingdom of God and the powers of evil. Reading Revelation from an idealist approach focuses on understanding God's perspective on the struggle between good and evil that exists in our world today.

Many historical premillennialists, amillennialists, and postmillennialists include aspects of idealism in their interpretations of Revelation.

Here's how someone reading from an idealist perspective might interpret parts of Revelation:

- The seven churches in the opening chapters symbolize types of churches—with their various faults, strengths, and hopes—that can be found in all ages throughout history and also today.
- The crowd in Revelation 7 and 14 is not literally 144,000 Jewish believers from the tribes of Israel but instead symbolizes all followers of Jesus on earth who endure persecution. (See James 1:1 and Galatians 6:16 for Christians being referred to as "twelve tribes" and "the Israel of God.")
- The pregnant woman in Revelation 12 represents all the faithful; her child is Christ, and the dragon is Satan, the persecutor of the church throughout the ages. The great dragon Satan was "hurled down" through the sacrificial and victorious death and resurrection of Christ (Revelation 12:9; John 12:31–33; 16:11).

- In Revelation 13, the beast from the sea represents, not one future Antichrist, but instead the wicked rulers and realms in every age who try to pervert God's plans and persecute God's people by demanding absolute allegiance. The forty-two months in which the beast exercises its power is not a literal time period but instead symbolizes any period of tribulation, the kind that has occurred since the resurrection of Jesus and will continue until he returns.

Preterist View

If you see the biblical apocalypses as writings that mostly tell about events surrounding the time period in which the texts were written, that's a *preterist* perspective. The word *preterist* comes from the Latin *praeteritus*, which means "past" or "bygone."

Revelation is like a long-lost newspaper from the past.

In this view, most or all of the events in Revelation have already happened either around the time John received his heavenly visions or a few decades earlier. Bible scholars generally agree that the apostle John wrote Revelation, but pinpointing exactly when is far less certain. They have proposed two main options, either during the reign of Roman Emperor Nero (AD 54–68) or that of Emperor Domitian (AD 81–96). Both emperors were known to persecute Christians. In AD 70 during the Jewish-Roman war, the Roman army destroyed the Jewish temple in Jerusalem. In the preterist perspective, the visions in Revelation reflect events surrounding the fall of Jerusalem, the destruction of the temple, persecutions of Christians, and other first-century atrocities.

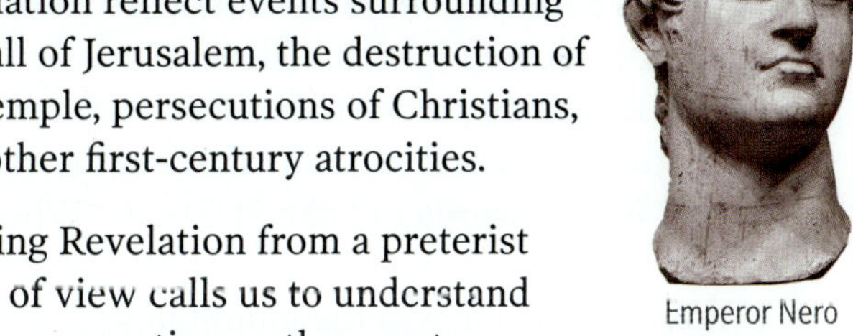
Emperor Nero

Reading Revelation from a preterist point of view calls us to understand God's perspective on the events that many of the first followers of Jesus endured, which Jesus described and which he warned his followers to be ready for. Historical premillennialists, amillennialists, and postmillennialists are sometimes also "partial preterists," which means that they see much of Revelation as fulfilled in the first century while still recognizing that the final chapters will not be fulfilled until the end of time.

From this standpoint, here is how some of John's visions might be interpreted:

- The violence and devastation that comes from opening the seals in Revelation 6 and sounding the trumpets in Revelation 8 are depictions of the first-century Roman war against the Jewish Revolt in Judea.

- The crowd of 144,000 in Revelation 7 might refer to the Jewish Christians who fled Judea during or just before the war.
- The pregnant woman in Revelation 12 is faithful Israel who gave birth to Jesus Christ. Satan (the dragon) persecuted Jewish believers in Jesus through Roman oppression, but they escaped the destruction of Jerusalem in the first century by heeding Jesus's words in Luke 21:20–22: "When you see Jerusalem being surrounded by armies ... let those in Judea flee to the mountains."
- The beast from the sea in Revelation 13 was Emperor Nero who severely persecuted Christians for approximately forty-two months, from the autumn of AD 64 to the late spring of AD 68. When spelled in Hebrew letters, "Nero Caesar" adds up to 666.
- The beast from the earth in Revelation 13 is one of the false prophets who lead people astray before the destruction of the temple which Jesus warned about: "Many false prophets will appear and deceive many people" (Matthew 24:11).

Waiting for a New Day

It's important to notice that none of these four approaches to Revelation completely excludes the others. The biblical writers mixed literary genres, and nearly every interpreter today draws from more than one of the four approaches when reading biblical apocalypses.

In fact, all Christians understand the final chapters of the book (Revelation 20 and 21) from a futurist standpoint, even if they take very different approaches to the rest of the book. All believers in Jesus are waiting to behold the new heaven and new earth that John witnessed. That day will be a glorious day when, as John records, "God himself will be with them and ... will wipe every tear from their eyes. There will be no more death or mourning or crying or pain, for the old order of things has passed" (Revelation 21:3–4).

The book of Revelation opens with a promise that all who will read it and take its words to heart will be blessed (Revelation 1:3). No matter which of the approaches you land on or how you understand the various details of the visions, the words of Revelation are worth reading, studying, and taking to heart.

John closes the book with a prayer that can be echoed by anyone awaiting the glorious return of King Jesus: "Amen. Come Lord Jesus."

FUTURIST VIEW	Revelation tells what will happen in the future, leading up to and during the end times. Apocalyptic writings in the Bible are read as predictive prophecies about events that are yet to occur.
HISTORICIST VIEW	Revelation tells what is happening from God's perspective throughout a particular period of history. Apocalyptic writings in the Bible are read as retellings of certain epochs of history.
IDEALIST VIEW	Revelation tells in picturesque language the conflict that is always happening between good and evil. Apocalyptic writings in the Bible are read as symbolic expressions of struggles between good and evil that occur in every age.
PRETERIST VIEW	Revelation tells about events that happened in the first century, around the time that John wrote the book. Apocalyptic writings in the Bible are read as elaborate descriptions of historical events that occurred near the time they were written.

CHAPTER 4

What Did Jesus Say about the End Times?

Jesus talked a lot about the end times—and no wonder! Jesus is the beginning and the end, the source and the goal of God's work in human history. The future has a name—and that name is Jesus.

Most of what Jesus told his first followers about the end times didn't take the form of lectures or discourses; he mostly told parables. Parables are analogies in the form of short stories that convey a particular point about God's work. Jesus told his disciples about:

- **A field** where weeds and wheat grew together because an evil neighbor had tossed weed seed into the field; the wheat and the weeds remained together until harvest time when they were separated (Matthew 13:24–43).

- **A net** that caught every kind of seafood; the good fish were saved in baskets while the bad ones were thrown away (Matthew 13:47–50).
- **A king** whose invited guests rejected his invitation to the crown prince's wedding banquet; the king then welcomed anyone he could find to attend—good and bad guests. But when an ill-prepared guest crashed the feast, the king had him thrown out of the party (Matthew 22:1–14).
- **Five bridesmaids** who missed the bridegroom's arrival because they were unprepared by not bringing enough olive oil for their lamps; the other five bridesmaids who were prepared were welcomed into the wedding banquet (Matthew 25:1–13).
- **Three servants** who were either glorified or condemned based on what they had done with the money their master entrusted to them while he was away on a long journey (Matthew 25:14–30).
- **People from all nations** who were separated "as a shepherd separates the sheep from the goats" based on how they had responded to those in need (Matthew 25:31–46).

What do these teachings of Jesus tell us about the end times? Here are three truths that come directly from these parables:

1. Jesus will return.

In the parable of the bridesmaids, Jesus (the bridegroom) arrives "after a long time" (Matthew 25:10). In the story about the sheep and the goats, the Son of Man returns "in his glory" (Matthew 25:31).

2. No one knows when Jesus will return.

Before telling the story of the bridesmaids who ran out of oil, Jesus made it clear that no one would be able to know the time of his return: "But about that day or hour no one knows, not even the angels in heaven, nor the Son, but only the Father" (Matthew 24:36). The angels don't know. The disciples don't know. In fact, during his time on earth, not even Jesus knew when he would return! He concluded the parable of the bridesmaids by urging his disciples to "therefore, keep watch, because you do not know the day or the hour" (Matthew 25:13).

3. There will be a final judgment.

After separating the wheat from the weeds, the angels throw the weeds into a fiery place where the condemned will grind their teeth and cry in agony. A similar fate meets the bad fish, the wedding crasher, the servant who kept his master's money to himself, and the goats who rejected helping the brothers and sisters of Jesus.

When it comes to those three points about the end times, everyone who trusts the truth of Scripture can find common ground.

The Olivet Discourse

Once, Jesus taught about the end of time through a prophecy instead of a parable. This prophetic teaching took place on the Mount of Olives just beyond the walls of Jerusalem, only days before Jesus went to the cross.

Here's what happened: As Jesus left the temple courts, a few of his followers pointed out the splendor of the temple that King Herod had renovated to be the most magnificent building in Jerusalem. Jesus responded by predicting the unthinkable: *the temple would be destroyed.*

> *"Do you see all these things?... Truly I tell you, not one stone here will be left on another; every one will be thrown down."* (Matthew 24:2)

When they reached the Mount of Olives, the disciples asked Jesus, "Tell us ... when will this happen, and what will be the sign of your coming and of the end of the age?" (Matthew 24:3). Jesus revealed to them a series of events that were, for him and his first followers, still in the future. Because his words were spoken on the Mount of Olives, this extended teaching is known as the Olivet Discourse. It's included in three of the Gospels: Matthew 24; Mark 13; Luke 21.

Jesus told his disciples on the Mount of Olives that

- False messiahs and false prophets will come in his name and deceive many people. There will be wars and rumors of wars, famines, earthquakes, and pestilences. Followers of Jesus will be betrayed, hated, imprisoned, and put on trial, but the Holy Spirit will guide them. Despite persecution, the gospel will be preached in the whole world (Matthew 24:4–14, 23–26; Mark 13:5–9, 21–23; Luke 21:8–16).

- When the "abomination that causes desolation" stands in the holy place, those in Judea should immediately flee to the mountains (Matthew 24:15–20; Mark 13:14–18; Luke 21:20–23).

- The world will see "great distress" like it has never seen before. Jerusalem will be surrounded by armies and trampled on by gentiles (Matthew 24:21–25; Mark 13:19–20; Luke 21:20–24).

- The sun and moon will become dark, and the stars will fall from the sky (Matthew 24:29; Mark 13:24–25; Luke 21:25–26).

- All people will see the Son of Man coming in the clouds with power and glory. Then the elect will be gathered from the earth (Matthew 24:30–31; Mark 13:26–27; Luke 21:27–28).

- This generation will not pass away until all these events have happened (Matthew 24:32–35; Mark 13:28–31; Luke 21:29–36).

While no one knows exactly when the Lord will return (Jesus was very clear on that point), still, Bible readers today are left wondering *how far* into the future are (or were) the events of the Olivet Discourse.

- Were the events only a literal generation away, things that the disciples would personally experience in their lifetimes?

- Are the events far into the future, closer to the time when Jesus returns to earth?

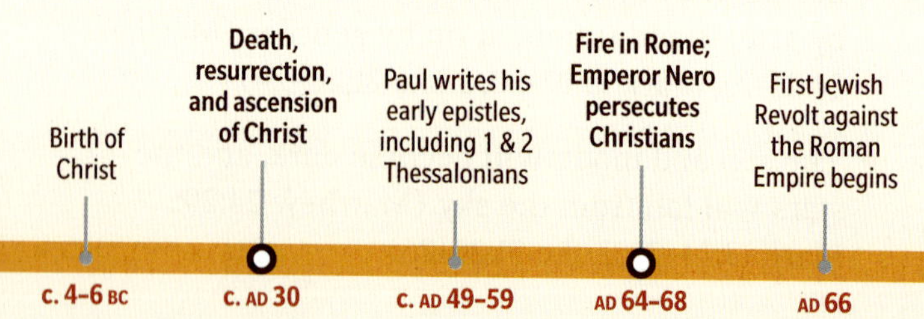

- Or maybe both: Did Jesus's discourse predict first-century events as well as ones that will happen in the end of time just before he returns?

Sincere, Bible-believing Christians differ on how to answer these questions. There are two main ways that Christians read these words from Jesus on the Mount of Olives. Some focus on the end times, while others focus on the first century. Let's look at how each focus results in different understandings of what Jesus said.

➤ Focus on the End Times

From this perspective, readers see Jesus's words primarily as descriptions of events that will happen in the end times. Jesus did predict the destruction of the temple in the first century, however, his focus in the discourse was on the calamities at the beginning of the future tribulation and on the Antichrist's sacrilege in a Jewish temple that will be rebuilt during the seven-

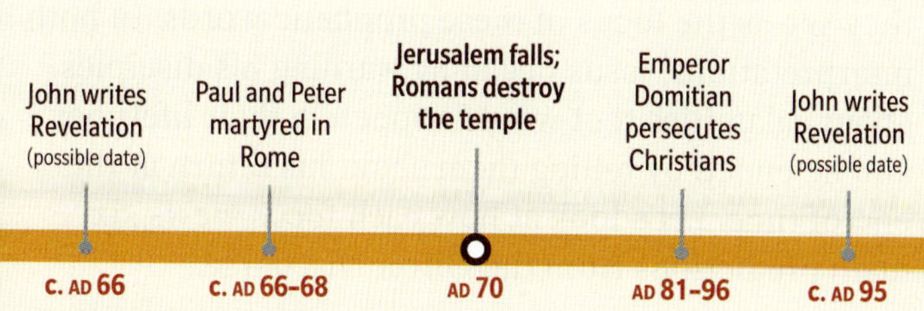

year tribulation, followed by the return of the Son of Man to the earth. Therefore, Christians today still await these events.

Dispensational premillennialists and some historical premillennialists read the Olivet Discourse from this viewpoint.

Focus on the First Century

In this perspective, most of the events in the Olivet Discourse were fulfilled in the first century. Jesus, therefore, was warning his disciples about what would happen in their lifetimes, particularly regarding events surrounding the destruction of the temple, which would occur about four decades after Jesus.

Amillennialists, postmillennialists, and many historical premillennialists often read the Olivet Discourse from this viewpoint.

Both perspectives agree that Jesus predicted the destruction of the Jerusalem temple in AD 70 and that the last part of his Olivet Discourse describes the end of time. Where the two perspectives differ is in what they see as the focus of these prophetic words. In both interpretations, Jesus began by warning his disciples about calamities that would happen in their lifetimes, and he ended by telling them about his return at the end of time. Let's look at how each focus views six main predictions from the Olivet Discourse.

Wars, Natural Disasters, Persecution, and False Messiahs

"Many will come in my name, claiming, 'I am the Messiah,' and will deceive many. You will hear of wars and rumors of wars, but see to it that you are not alarmed. Such things must happen, but the end is still to come. Nation will rise against nation, and kingdom against kingdom. There will be famines and earthquakes in various places. All these are the beginning of birth pains.... Then you will be handed over to be persecuted and put to death."

MATTHEW 24:5–7, 9

➤ Focus on the End Times

Natural disasters, wars, the persecution of Christians, and the arrival of false messiahs and false prophets even from within the church—all of these things describe the era either immediately before a future tribulation or during the early part of this tribulation.

According to dispensationalists, Jesus will remove his church from the world in the rapture before (or partway through) this seven-year tribulation.

Some readers see parallels between the Olivet Discourse and the book of Revelation.[5]

	MATTHEW 24	REVELATION 6
Antichrist	"Many will come in my name, claiming 'I am the Messiah,' and will deceive many" (v. 5).	The rider on the white horse "was given a crown, and he rode out as a conqueror bent on conquest" (v. 2).
Wars	"You will hear of wars and rumors of wars" (v. 6).	The rider on the red horse "was given power to take peace from the earth and to make people kill each other" (v. 4).
Famine	"There will be famines" (v. 7).	The rider on the black horse holds a pair of scales, indicating food scarcity (v. 5–6).
Disasters	"There will be ... earthquakes" (v. 7) and "pestilences in various places" (Luke 21:11).	The rider on the pale horse brings death "by sword and plague, and by the wild beasts" (v. 8).
Martyrdom	"You will be handed over to be persecuted and put to death" (v. 9).	John sees the "souls of those who had been slain because of the word of God and the testimony they maintained" (v. 9).

➤ Focus on the First Century

The "wars and rumors of wars" were conflicts that broke out in AD 66 between the Romans and roving bands of Jewish revolutionaries. Two years later, Emperor Nero committed suicide, then three other emperors rose and fell amid a violent civil war. Under Emperor Vespasian and later his son Titus, Roman legions arrived in Galilee and swept southward toward Jerusalem, crushing the Jewish rebellion. The Jewish historian Josephus wrote that on the shores of the Sea of Galilee "one could see the whole lake red with blood and covered with corpses, for not a man escaped."[6]

A Christian prophet predicted a famine that occurred in the late 40s during the reign of Emperor Claudius (Acts 11:28). An earthquake rocked Pompeii and Herculaneum in AD 62. The philosopher Seneca, writing in the mid-60s, described how earthquakes had obliterated twelve cities in Asia Minor.[7] Josephus reported a severe quaking of the earth around Jerusalem not long before the Jerusalem fell to the Romans.[8]

"You will be handed over to be persecuted" may refer to Emperor Nero's persecution of Christians. After a fire in Rome in AD 64, Nero viciously attacked Christians in and around the city. The apostle Peter was martyred during this period of persecution.

Twelve years after Jesus warned about "false messiahs and false prophets," a self-proclaimed prophet named Theudas led hundreds to their deaths (Acts 5:36). Later, an unnamed Egyptian and his followers met a similar fate (Acts 21:38).

2 The Abomination in the Holy Place

> *"So when you see standing in the holy place 'the abomination that causes desolation,' spoken of through the prophet Daniel—let the reader understand—then let those who are in Judea flee to the mountains."*
>
> MATTHEW 24:15–16

➤ Focus on the End Times

The phrase "abomination that causes desolation" comes from the Old Testament prophet Daniel. In an apocalyptic vision, Daniel is told by an angel that "the end will come like a flood; war will continue until the end" and someone would come who, at the temple, "will set up an abomination that causes desolation, until the end that is decreed is poured out on him" (Daniel 9:26–27).

Dispensationalists see this as the Antichrist, who will enter the rebuilt temple ("the holy place") and proclaim himself to be divine. This proclamation will occur halfway through the seven-year tribulation. This sacrilegious act will mark the beginning of the great tribulation, which is the second half of the tribulation (2 Thessalonians 2:3–9; Revelation 13). Jesus was warning future Jewish believers who may be in Israel during the tribulation to flee to the hills when this event occurs. The worst of God's wrath will then fall on the earth during this latter part of the tribulation.

➤ Focus on the First Century

"The holy place" could refer to the first-century Jewish temple or, more broadly, to the entire promised land.[9] The "abomination" is a sacrilegious event that occurs in the middle of Daniel's "seventieth seven" (Daniel 9:27). Early Christian leaders ranging from Eusebius and Athanasius to John Chrysostom and Clement of Alexandria connected this abomination with the events leading up to the destruction of the temple in the first century. Here are some possibilities:

- The abomination could have been the religious leaders' rejection of Jesus, the true temple of God (John 2:13–22). This abominable rejection resulted in the "desolation" of the Jewish temple.
- The abomination could have been the Jewish violation of the temple during the Roman siege. Seeking to strengthen their own position against

other factions from their own people, some among the Jewish rebels, as Josephus explained, made "the temple a receptacle of all wickedness so that the divine place has now become polluted by the hands of our own people." Shortly before the fall of Jerusalem, the rebel leader John of Gischala "took to sacrilege" by melting down the precious temple vessels to enrich himself.[10]

- The abomination could have been the Roman violation of Judea, Jerusalem, and the temple. Throughout their conquest and siege, the Romans carried pagan ensigns or standards and sacrificed to them. The Roman soldiers set up their ensigns in the temple and celebrated their victory with sacrifices. According to a later Jewish source, the

The Siege and Destruction of Jerusalem (David Roberts, c. 1850)

> commander of the Roman army even entered the most sacred place of the temple and committed fornication with a harlot atop an unrolled scroll of the Hebrew Scriptures.[11]

Jesus warned his followers to flee Judea when they saw signs of this coming desolation—and that's precisely what they did. Josephus described how people slipped out of the besieged city, beginning in AD 66 and continuing through the weeks immediately prior to the fall of Jerusalem. According to several ancient sources, members of the Jerusalem church had received a divine warning before the revolt, telling them to leave the city.[12]

3 The Great Distress

> *"For then there will be great distress, unequaled from the beginning of the world until now—and never to be equaled again.... For as lightning that comes from the east is visible even in the west, so will be the coming of the Son of Man."*
>
> MATTHEW 24:21–27

➤ Focus on the End Times

Dispensationalists typically see the forty-two months mentioned in Revelation 11:2 as the first half of the seven-year tribulation, when the gentiles will "trample on the holy city." Revelation 13:5 describes the second half of the tribulation, when the beast from the sea (the Antichrist) is given the power to speak blasphemies and exercise authority. This second half of the tribulation is the great tribulation or great distress that Jesus predicted.

The tribulation will end when Jesus returns personally and visibly to earth. His second coming will "cut short" the "days of distress" for the sake of God's elect (Mark 13:18–20). Both dispensational and historical premillennialists understand the arrival of Christ at the end of the tribulation as the time when he will defeat every power of darkness in the battle of Armageddon and then establish his millennial kingdom.

Focus on the First Century

Interpretations vary about how long the great distress (or great tribulation) was or is.

Some believe the tribulation was fulfilled in the years leading up to the destruction of the temple in Jerusalem. During this time, the location where God had chosen "to put his Name" (Deuteronomy 12:5) was profaned in ways that had never happened before and will never happen again.

THE ARRIVAL OF THE LORD

The imagery of lightning comes from the prophecies of Zechariah 9:14–17 and points to God arriving on the scene like a mighty warrior to save his people: "Then the LORD will appear over them; his arrow will flash like lightning. The Sovereign LORD will sound the trumpet; he will march in the storms of the south" (verse 14).

Others, however, see this time of distress as far longer. In this view, the tribulation began in the first century and continues to today—and it will continue until Jesus returns. In other words, it began with the first-century siege of Jerusalem (past) but will continue until Jesus's second coming (future). Throughout this time of tribulation in which we now live, evil will continue to multiply until Jesus returns and destroys the dominion of the devil.

The "coming of the Son of Man"—which will be as visible as lightning—may be either a symbolic reference to God's judgment on Israel in AD 70 (past) or the return of Jesus to earth immediately before time ends and eternity begins (future).

Sun and Moon Darkened, and Stars Fall

"Immediately after the distress of those days 'the sun will be darkened, and the moon will not give its light; the stars will fall from the sky, and the heavenly bodies will be shaken.'"

MATTHEW 24:29

➤ Focus on the End Times

Jesus's words in this prediction echo the words of Isaiah 13:10; 34:4. No matter which of the four millennial views one holds, nearly all understand Matthew 24:29 as referring to the judgment that Christ will bring when he returns to earth. But the viewpoints differ on how literally or how figuratively to interpret the prediction.

Some interpreters expect real cosmic catastrophes to accompany the Messiah's second coming. They also see this text as referring to the same event John described in Revelation 19:11–16, where the "King of Kings and Lord of Lords" is riding on a white horse and leveling judgment upon the nations.

Others take the description of the sun, moon, and stars figuratively. When Jesus said, "after the distress of those days," he was describing a time after the tribulation using terms drawn from the ancient

Hebrew prophets. In the Old Testament, images of darkened or shaking celestial bodies symbolize divine judgment upon a nation:

- Isaiah predicted the fall of Babylon, which occurred in 539 BC, saying, “The stars ... will not show their light. The rising sun will be darkened and the moon will not give its light” (Isaiah 13:10).
- When Isaiah portrayed Egypt’s crumbling power in the seventh and sixth centuries BC, he stated that “the LORD rides on a swift cloud” (Isaiah 19:1).
- In the book of Ezekiel, God says about Egypt in the aftermath of the death of Pharaoh, “I will cover the heavens and darken their stars; I will cover the sun with a cloud, and the moon will not give its light” (Ezekiel 32:7–8).

It is unlikely that God physically flew around on a cloud in the atmosphere above Africa as Egypt’s power faltered, or that the sun, moon, and stars stopped giving light when Babylon fell. So perhaps Jesus did not intend his words in the Olivet Discourse to literally mean that stars would fall and the sun and moon would stop shining. Instead, he was using the familiar language of the prophets to describe a future decisive judgment from God.

Either way, most interpreters agree that these verses describe events leading up to the end of time.

➤ Focus on the First Century

Some preterist interpreters see this prediction as a symbolic description of divine judgment on the Jewish people in AD 70.

5 The Sign of the Son of Man

"Then will appear the sign of the Son of Man in heaven. And then all the peoples of the earth will mourn when they see the Son of Man coming on the clouds of heaven, with power and great glory. And he will send his angels with a loud trumpet call, and they will gather his elect from the four winds, from one end of the heavens to the other."

MATTHEW 24:30–31

➤ Focus on the End Times

The words of Jesus translated in Matthew 24:30 as "peoples of the earth" can also be rendered "tribes of the land." From a dispensationalist view, these words refer to the Jewish people. Near the end of the seven-year tribulation, the nations of the earth will unite against Israel, culminating in the battle of Armageddon. As these armies close in on Israel, the Jewish people will repent ("mourn") and finally recognize Jesus as their Messiah.

The "sign of the Son of Man" will be the glorious appearing of Christ. He will destroy the enemies of Israel and gather everyone who trusts him ("his elect from the four winds").

Zechariah foresaw this event in the Old Testament and described his vision with these words from the Lord:

> *On that day I will set out to destroy all the nations that attack Jerusalem. And I will pour out on the house of David and the inhabitants of Jerusalem a spirit of grace and supplication. They will look on me, the one they have pierced, and they will mourn for him as one mourns for an only child, and grieve bitterly as one grieves for a firstborn son. On that day the weeping in Jerusalem will be as great as the weeping of Hadad Rimmon in the plain of Megiddo.* (Zechariah 12:9–11)

➤ Focus on the First Century

Other end-times views agree with dispensationalists that Jesus's words echo Zechariah and that "all the peoples of the earth" probably refers to the Jewish people. However, they disagree on what the "time of mourning" and the "sign of the Son of Man" mean.

Some suggest that these moments of mourning took place in the first century. If so, the "Son of Man coming on the clouds of heaven" is a metaphor for God's judgment on Israel, similar to Isaiah's description of God's judgment on Egypt (Isaiah 19:1). After Jerusalem fell to the Romans, God began to gather his people primarily from among the gentiles. This gathering will continue until a great multitude of gentiles comes to faith in Jesus (Romans 11:25). Understood in this way, Jesus was not talking about his return at all. He was describing the implications of the destruction of the temple in AD 70.

What in the year 70 could possibly have been a "coming" and a "sign" that people could see? Some people in Judea did attest to a series of strange and miraculous signs that marked the fall of the temple. Here's how Josephus described these occurrences:

> *I suppose this account would seem to be false except that eye-witnesses vouched for it:... Before sunset, chariots were seen in the air over the whole land, and armored soldiers were speeding through the clouds and encircling the cities.... As the priests were going by night into the inner court, they felt a quaking and heard a great noise. After that, they heard a sound something like a large crowd saying, "Let us leave this place."*[13]

The Roman historian Tacitus described a moment when

> *in the sky, there appeared a vision of armies in glittering armor in conflict. Then a lightning flash*

> *from the clouds illuminated the temple! The doors of this holy place suddenly opened, a superhuman voice was heard declaring that the gods were leaving, and at the same time came the sound of a rushing tumult.*[14]

In light of these reports, it's possible that a visible sign of the Son of Man did appear in the clouds of heaven in the first century.

Another interpretation of Jesus's words is that he was speaking both of past and future events. The great tribulation is seen as an era which began with the Roman persecution of Christians (past) and which will continue until Jesus returns (future). Christ will be revealed and will return to earth "immediately after the distress of those days," just as he predicted (Matthew 24:29). The "mourning" represents the response of the Jewish people at the end of time when they recognize how their ancestors rejected Israel's Messiah (Zechariah 12:9–14; Romans 11:17–27). Although supernatural signs were seen in the skies when the temple fell, none qualifies—according to some interpreters—as Christ coming in power and great glory.

6 This Generation

"Now learn this lesson from the fig tree: As soon as its twigs get tender and its leaves come out, you know that summer is near. When you see all these things, you know that it is near, right at the door. Truly I tell you, this generation will certainly not pass away until all these things have happened."

MATTHEW 24:32–34

➤ Focus on the End Times

According to some dispensationalists, "this generation" refers to the generation that will be on earth during the great tribulation. If that's the meaning of "this generation," Jesus was telling his disciples that those who will be living during the great tribulation are the people who will see the return of Jesus to the earth.[15]

Other dispensationalists, however, see the blooming of the fig tree as a symbol of the establishment of the modern nation of Israel in 1948—or perhaps of the Six Day War in 1967. If so, the tribulation will occur in the lifetimes of people who were alive in 1948 or 1967.[16] Therefore, the generation who witnessed the establishment of the modern nation of Israel will be the ones who will see the tribulation and the return of Christ.

➤ Focus on the First Century

According to some, "this generation" refers only to the people who were alive when Jesus spoke these words. The typical measure of a generation in the Old Testament was forty years (see Numbers 14:34). Jesus gave the Olivet Discourse around AD 30, so AD 70 was almost exactly a generation away. The phrase "all these things" would then refer to the destruction of the temple and all the unrest surrounding the Roman-Jewish war.

According to others, "this generation" is the church in every age. Writing to churches in the first century, the apostle Peter said, "You are a chosen people, a royal priesthood, a holy nation, God's special possession" (1 Peter 2:9). John Chrysostom, a pastor in the fourth century, understood "this generation" as a reference to the church age, so this interpretation does have a long history.[17] If that was the intent of Jesus's words, what Jesus was declaring was that no persecution or tribulation would destroy the church; the church will persist until his return, when the last of these prophecies will finally be fulfilled.

BEING READY FOR THE END TIMES

After Jesus's resurrection, when the disciples demanded details about when he would establish the kingdom, he replied,

> *It is not for you to know times or dates that the Father has set by his own authority.* (Acts 1:7)

Then, Jesus immediately reminded his followers of their responsibility to share with everyone what they had seen in him:

> *You will be my witnesses ... to the ends of the earth.* (Acts 1:8)

Jesus turned their attention from worrying about "times or dates" and focused it on their commission to proclaim the gospel.

The words translated into English as "times" and "dates" in this passage are two Greek words:

- *Times* translates a form of the Greek word *chronos,* which points to chronological, linear time as measured by a calendar, sundial, or clock; *chronos* includes years, months, days, and hours.
- *Dates* (or *seasons*) translates a form of the Greek word *kairos,* a word that points to the quality or type of time; the focus of *kairos* is on the opportunity or significance of a particular time.

By using both terms, Jesus made it clear that not only was it not the disciples' place to know when he would return, but also they wouldn't necessarily even know what type of time it would be when he returned.

Even after Jesus vanished into the eastern sky, his followers struggled with issues related to his return. Twenty years or so after Jesus's ascension, someone forged a letter in Paul's name and claimed to the Thessalonian church that Jesus had already returned (2 Thessalonians 2:2; 3:17). Not surprisingly, the thought that they might have missed their Savior's return caused quite a stir among the Christians in Thessalonica.

Paul responded by stating that the day of the Lord had certainly not yet occurred:

> *Concerning the coming of our Lord Jesus Christ and our being gathered to him, we ask you, brothers and sisters, not to become easily unsettled or alarmed by the teaching allegedly from us—whether by a prophecy or by word of mouth or by letter—asserting that the day of the Lord has already come. Don't let anyone deceive you in any way.*
> (2 Thessalonians 2:1–3)

Paul then wrote that before the second coming, there would be a rebellion of humanity against God and a revelation of a lawless man. Yet Paul did not dwell long on the details. In fact, he spent fewer than a dozen verses on these issues. Paul's purpose was not to drive the Thessalonians to speculate about who the man of lawlessness might be or when the rebellion might come; it was, instead, that "our Lord Jesus Christ himself and God our Father" would "encourage [their] hearts and strengthen [them] in every good deed and word" (2 Thessalonians 2:16–17).

Paul wasn't afraid to talk about the end times, but he knew that the end times are not the endpoint of God's plan. The endpoint of God's plan is Jesus Christ himself, and there will be a day when all things are brought into submission to Jesus (Philippians 2:10–11). And so, Paul called Christians to rest assured and to find comfort in God's promise that one day—no matter when that day may come—all things will be made new.

Do you notice a pattern? The focus in each of these end-times Bible passages is not on the details of how time might end. Some future occurrences are certainly described. And yet, again and again, the emphasis is on the sufficiency of Jesus, the one through whom God will bring about the end in his own time. Jesus is the goal of God's plan and the ultimate sign of God's work in human history. Because Jesus perfectly fulfilled his Father's will, the last days are already underway, and God's triumph is guaranteed.

Notes

1 Adapted from Graeme Goldsworthy, *Gospel and Kingdom* (Paternoster, 1994), chapter 5.

2 W. Percy, *The Message in the Bottle* repr. Ed. (Picador, 2000) 6, cited in R. Moore, "Personal and Cosmic Eschatology," in *A Theology for the Church*, ed. D. Akin (B&H Academic, 2007), 923.

3 Papias, *Fragments*; Justin Martyr, *Dialogue with Trypho*, 80, 110; Irenaeus, *Against Heresies*, 5:26; 5:30; 5:33; Tertullian, *Against Marcion*, 3:25 and *On the Resurrection of the Flesh*, 25.

4 Tim LaHaye, "One Hundred Forty-Four Thousand," *The Popular Encyclopedia of Biblical Prophecy* (Harvest House, 2004), 256–257.

5 Wayne House and Randall Price, *Charts of Bible Prophecy* (Zondervan, 2003), 130.

6 Josephus, *The Jewish War*, 3:10:9.

7 Seneca, *Natural Questions*, 6:1–11.

8 Josephus, *The Jewish War*, 6:5:3.

9 See 2 Maccabees 2:18, where a Jewish writer refers to the whole land as "the holy place."

10 Josephus, *The Jewish War*, 5:9:4; 5:13:6.

11 Babylonian Talmud, Gittin 56b (9).

12 Athanasius, *Defense of His Flight*, 11; John Chrysostom, *Homilies*, 75:2, 76:1; Clement, *Homilies*, 3:15; Josephus, *The Jewish War*, 2:20:1, 4:6:1, 4:7:3, 5:10:1, 5:13:4, 6:2:2, 6:6:1; Eusebius, *Church History*, 3:5; Epiphanius, *On Weights and Measures*, 15; Abot de Rabbi Nathan (Brill, 1975), 67–69.

13 Josephus, *The Jewish War*, 6:5:3.

14 Tacitus, *Annals*, 5:13.

15 John Walvoord, *Prophecy Knowledge Handbook* (Victor Books, 1990), 391.

16 Walvoord, *Prophecy Knowledge Handbook*, 391; Hal Lindsey, *The Late Great Planet Earth* (Zondervan, 1970), 53.

17 Chrysostom, *Homilies*, 49.

MADE EASY

by Rose Publishing

BIBLE STUDY MADE EASY
A step-by-step guide to studying God's Word

HOW WE GOT THE BIBLE MADE EASY
Key events in the history of the Bible

UNDERSTANDING THE HOLY SPIRIT MADE EASY
Who the Holy Spirit is and what he does

BIBLE CHRONOLOGY MADE EASY
Bible characters and events in the order they happened

THE BOOKS OF THE BIBLE MADE EASY
Quick summaries of all 66 books of the Bible

KNOWING GOD'S WILL MADE EASY
Answers to tough questions about God's will

WORLD RELIGIONS MADE EASY
30 religions and how they compare to Christianity

BASICS OF THE CHRISTIAN FAITH MADE EASY
Key Christian beliefs and practices

SHARING YOUR FAITH MADE EASY
How to share the gospel

BIBLE TRANSLATIONS MADE EASY
Compares 20 popular Bible versions

BOOK OF REVELATION
Who, what, where, when, and why of Revelation

WHO'S WHO IN THE BIBLE
Key facts about the Bible's main characters

SCRIPTURE MEMORY MADE EASY
Strategies for hiding God's Word in your heart

END TIMES MADE EASY
Presents key Christian views of the End Times

www.hendricksonrose.com